The Be-Attitudes

Eight Studies For Adult Individuals or Groups

How We Can Get Over Ourselves And Live Lives Approved By God!

S.A. Keith

The Be-Attitudes
How We Can Get Over Ourselves And
Live Lives Approved By God!

ISBN: 978-0-9665124-2-7

Copyright 2006 S.A. Keith
ALL RIGHTS RESERVED

Bible-4-Life.com

No part of this book may be reproduced in any form without written permission from S.A. Keith.

Unless otherwise indicated, Bible references are from the New International Version.

Editor: Kit MacLeod

Bible-4-Life.com
438 East Ilex Drive
Lake Park, FL 33403
Email: info@Bible-4-Life.com

The Be-Attitudes
How We Can Get Over Ourselves And
Live Lives Approved By God!

I lovingly dedicate this book to my husband, Bob.
His life-struggle inspired the writing of this book.
Like Jesus, Bob has been a man of sorrow
and acquainted with grief.

I especially want to thank Elizabeth Nielsen
and the J.A.Y. Women's Bible Study Group
for their helpful insights.

And as always,
to my wonderful friend and editor,
Kit MacLeod,
for helping me to write better than I do!

The Be-Attitudes
How We Can Get Over Ourselves And
Live Lives Approved By God!

*"Have this attitude in yourselves which
was also in Christ Jesus…" Philippians 2:5 (NAS)*

Contents

1. The BE-Attitudes	5
2. Blessed are the poor in spirit…	9
3. Blessed are those who mourn…	15
4. Blessed are the meek…	26
5. Blessed are those who hunger and thirst for righteousness…	32
6. Blessed are the merciful…	38
7. Blessed are the pure in heart…	44
8. Blessed are the peacemakers…	50
9. Blessed are those who are persecuted because of righteousness…	55

The Be-Attitudes
How We Can Get Over Ourselves And
Live Lives Approved By God!

"I just can't get over it!"

Most of us, if not all of us, at one time or another have to deal with experiences in our past or current life which make us stumble in our faith or that cripple us emotionally. It could be something as severe as being abused as a child or as simple as a feeling that our parents didn't give us the attention we needed growing up. Maybe it's a broken friendship or business plan gone sour. Whatever "it" is, many times these painful experiences can affect us the rest of our lives and prevent us from reaching our greatest potential, or even end up destroying us. Trying to "get over it" doesn't work. We try and fail and "it" goes round and round in our minds, blocking us from receiving what God intends for our lives. Thankfully, there is an alternative. God can heal our pain so that we can live a productive, God-approved life.

The Be-Attitudes
How We Can Get Over Ourselves And Live Lives Approved By God!

This series has been written with the hope and prayer that it will help those who feel powerless to overcome their pain. I hope that this will help you unlock the key to spiritual and emotional healing and to "get over" the painful experiences in life - past, present, and all that life may throw at you in the future.

The Beatitudes are the eight declarations made by Jesus at the beginning of his Sermon on the Mount, recorded in Matthew 5:3-12. Each one begins with the words, "Blessed are", and continues with a statement concerning those who live in obedient and joyful unity with God. They are for those who partake in his salvation, and who have entered into his kingdom, not in its fullest sense, but as a foretaste of what's to come.

The word "blessed" has sometimes been translated as "happy". However, happiness most often depends on your current emotional situation. Therefore, the word "blessed" more accurately describes the spiritual harmony of a person who is in relationship with the King of the universe. This is

The Be-Attitudes
How We Can Get Over Ourselves And Live Lives Approved By God!

one who is approved by Him and who is secure in understanding that he shares a place in His eternal kingdom. As Christians we live in the "already and not yet" of God's kingdom. The Beatitudes teach us what it means to start the Kingdom-journey and are concerned with one's inner life and attitudes while here on earth. They teach us how to think and act and how to receive God's riches in order to become the salt of the earth and lights on a hill. They also tell us what rewards are in store for those who abide by them. God has a purpose and a plan for you. The Beatitudes, I believe, can help you discover that purpose and plan!

I confess that before embarking on this study, I had never closely studied the Beatitudes. I think I did what many people do; quickly reading through them to get to the "real meat" of Jesus' sermon. What a mistake that is, because unless you understand them, it is impossible to apply the rest of Jesus' sermon to your life.

I hope you'll use this series for personal Bible study or in a group setting, because these eight declarations are absolutely life-changing! My hope for you is to make the Beatitudes

The Be-Attitudes
How We Can Get Over Ourselves And Live Lives Approved By God!

your daily attitudes so you can become the person God intended you to be, and live your life approved by God!

Please Note: This eight session study is for adult individuals or groups. In group settings it is recommended that one person facilitates the discussion, but this isn't necessary. To further enhance your study time, I suggest looking up the Bible references marked, "Read" from different translations. The discussion questions can be worked together or done in private, then discussed.

In His Loving Grip,

S. A. Keith

The Be-Attitudes
How We Can Get Over Ourselves And
Live Lives Approved By God!

Blessed are the poor in spirit, for theirs is the kingdom of heaven.
Matthew 5:3

Since when has being poor a good thing? We want to be rich in spirit, rich in health and rich in our bank accounts! We want the best of everything, because having the best is a measurement of our success. Right? However, when Jesus began his sermon on the mount by saying, "Blessed are the poor in Spirit...", he was not touting the benefits of those who *don't* have money, nice clothing or fine food to eat. In God's economy, being poor in spirit is about emptiness -- spiritual emptiness. It is coming to the realization that we are powerless to help ourselves and that nothing in and of ourselves naturally chooses to follow God's ways.

The Be-Attitudes
How We Can Get Over Ourselves And Live Lives Approved By God!

"There is no one righteous, not even one; there is no one who understands, no one who seeks God. All have turned away, they have together become worthless; there is no one who does good, not even one." (Romans 3:10-12)

We can't work our way to earning God's favor and approval either.

"All of us have become like one who is unclean, and all our righteous acts are like filthy rags..." (Isaiah 64:6)

Another way to say Jesus' opening statement could be said like this, "Blessed, or approved by God, are the empty ones, for theirs is the kingdom of heaven." Being empty, or poor in spirit, is exactly what Jesus wants from us. Admitting our spiritual poverty is the beginning point to spiritual and emotional healing. God longs for us to see our emptiness and need for a Savior.

The Be-Attitudes
How We Can Get Over Ourselves And
Live Lives Approved By God!

"Have this attitude in yourselves which was also in Christ Jesus, who, although he existed in the form of God, did not regard equality with God a thing to be grasped, but emptied Himself, taking the form of a bond-servant, and being made in the likeness of men. And being found in appearance as a man, He humbled himself by becoming obedient to the point of death, even death on a cross." (Philippians 2:5-8 – NAS)

Think about this: Jesus had equal status with God, but he gave up all the privileges that come with being God to become a servant! Can you imagine this? He set aside his God-self, his deity, to become a lowly human-being! He did this for one purpose: to redeem the sons and daughters of Adam and Eve; who *wanted* equality with God, "to be like God", and by desiring to get it, disobeyed God.

Read: Genesis 3:1-7, 14-15.

I do not think it is an accident that the very thing Jesus

The Be-Attitudes
How We Can Get Over Ourselves And
Live Lives Approved By God!

requires from us, in order to be approved by God, is what he did when he came to earth to redeem us, to buy us back. He emptied himself, he became nothing, he became a man, a slave, to save us from death! Jesus asks us to do the same thing, *to have his same attitude* - to empty ourselves.

Verse 15 of Genesis predicts the future for our adversary, and for us, "I (God) will put enmity between you (Satan) and the woman (Eve), and between your offspring and hers (Eve's ancestors); he (Jesus) will crush your head, and you will strike his heel."

Our approval from God is totally dependent on the redemption which Jesus did on our behalf. Satan struck the heel of Jesus when he was crucified--for Jesus' followers, it appeared like all was lost--but the victory for all people is in the resurrection when Jesus crushed Satan by rising from the dead!

"Where, O death, is your victory?
Where, O death, is your sting?" 1 Corinthians 15:55

The Be-Attitudes
How We Can Get Over Ourselves And Live Lives Approved By God!

The way to be approved by God is by following Jesus' attitude: *he did not seek equality with God, but emptied himself …*

The immediate benefit of admitting to God that you are poor in Spirit, and that you cannot save yourself, is that he forgives *your* sins, fills you with his Spirit and you become an heir to his heavenly throne. You begin the journey. You have entered God's kingdom, but not in its fullest sense. That part comes when you see him face to face.

"Let the poor man say, 'I am rich in Him.'"

The Be-Attitudes
How We Can Get Over Ourselves And
Live Lives Approved By God!

Discussion Questions:

1) How would you define spiritual poverty?

2) What do the following references have to say about being "poor": Psalm 34:6; Psalm 40:17; 2 Corinthians 8:9; Revelation 3:17-21?

3) According to Philippians 2:5-8, what five Christ-like attitudes should believers possess?

4) According to Galatians 5:1, what happens when you don't empty yourself?

5) What blessings are in store for those who have admitted their spiritual poverty and are now filled with God's spirit? (See Psalm 84:10, John 15:1-5, Romans 8:35-39, Ephesians 1:3-8, 13-18, Hebrews 13:15.).

The Be-Attitudes
How We Can Get Over Ourselves And
Live Lives Approved By God!

Blessed are those who mourn, for they will be comforted. Matthew 5:4

"My God, my God, why have you forsaken me?"
(Matthew 27:46)

As Jesus hung dying on the cross he cried out, *"Why… me?"* At that pinnacle moment the full wrath of God descended on him, causing him to be totally and utterly separated from God's love.

When we mourn, we too can feel like God has abandoned us. We cry out, "Why me?" This is a legitimate response to suffering. Yet, Jesus knew the answer as to why he came to suffer and die – he did it to take our punishment. The Bible tells us that Jesus went to the cross for the joy that was set before him (Hebrews 12:2). It seems odd that he found joy in

The Be-Attitudes
How We Can Get Over Ourselves And Live Lives Approved By God!

suffering, but he knew his suffering had purpose. It provided our forgiveness; he was about the work of giving us our lives back. He loved us so much that it brought him joy to do it!

Part of our problem is that we, unlike Jesus, don't usually know why God has allowed pain and suffering to present its ugly self in our lives. It seems purposeless or cruel.

When we mourn, we need the supernatural comfort that only God can bring to us. Jesus knows that living on earth can be very painful. He realizes that our hopes and plans get crushed, friendships are ruined, our loved ones die, and this breaks our hearts.

We mourn because the world is not right. Sin has corrupted the planet. There is pain and sickness, death, decay and disease. The Bible says the entire creation groans in pain until the coming of Jesus (Romans 8:19). In fact, it is in our distress, in the midst of our mourning, where we can see how needy and poor in spirit we really are! (Psalm 18:6, 22:24, 84:2)

Let's look at two passages which speak to Jesus' mourning.

The Be-Attitudes
How We Can Get Over Ourselves And
Live Lives Approved By God!

The shortest and possibly most famous one is, "Jesus wept." He wept because one of his closest friends had just died.

Read: John 11:1-45

Lazarus is dead. His sisters, Mary and Martha, are mourning his loss. When Martha discovers Jesus is finally coming to help them, she runs out to meet him. Can't you hear her saying, "Why?" "If you had been here, things would have been different! I don't understand. You could have healed him! Why did you let him die?"

Then Mary comes out to meet Jesus and wants to know the same thing, "Why?" "If only you'd have been here..." "If only you'd cared!"

We want to know the same thing too. "God, why?" "If only you had healed my child." "If only you had given me parents that loved me." "If only *you* had cared enough to be here when I needed you the most!" "If only you had made me different from what I am." "If only..."

The Be-Attitudes
How We Can Get Over Ourselves And
Live Lives Approved By God!

When Jesus hears these questions, what does he do? He cries! Why does he cry? He certainly knew he'd raise Lazarus to life in just a few seconds. He could have scolded the women for their lack of faith, but he didn't. So why does he cry? It doesn't make any sense! Yet it makes perfect sense when you realize he cares. He understands. He knows this wasn't how life was supposed to be. He cries with them. He mourns sin's destructive results and the pain it caused in their lives.

Read: Luke 13:31-35

> *"Oh Jerusalem, Jerusalem...how I have longed to gather your children together, like a hen gathers her chicks under her wings, but you were not willing..."*

Do you hear Jesus' sorrow for Jerusalem? He mourned for something that wasn't to be. The tenderness of Jesus' words is contrasted with the starkness of their rejection of him: *they were not willing*.

The Be-Attitudes
How We Can Get Over Ourselves And Live Lives Approved By God!

We too mourn for hoped-for situations that will never happen; for relationships or plans that just aren't going to be. We must empty our hearts of mourning by pouring it out to God. Take time to mourn your pain, suffer your loss, and grieve your regrets; Jesus mourns with you. But be careful not to hold onto your pain and allow it to become an excuse for retreating from life. You just might be tempted to use your suffering to explain away your own shortcomings and sinful failures.

Have you ever thought, *"If this hadn't happened to me, then I could have been successful." "If this hadn't happened, then I would be happy." "If this hadn't happened, then life would be different, and I would be different." "If these things hadn't happened, then I could trust God."*

Why does suffering take us by surprise? Where do we get the idea that if we pray enough and trust enough, then we'll be suffer-free? It could be a result of our western entitlement mindset, but it certainly isn't what the Bible teaches us. Think of Isaac, whose father held a knife over his head; or Joseph, who was sold into slavery. And of course there's

The Be-Attitudes
How We Can Get Over Ourselves And
Live Lives Approved By God!

Job, who lost everything: his children, his health and his worldly possessions. What about Steven, Paul, Peter, and Jesus? Their lives ended in horrific ways. Why do we not expect to encounter the same? Is it false teaching or preaching that makes us think this way? Maybe, but maybe it's a remnant memory which God programmed into our hearts at creation, because it wasn't supposed to be like this. We were created to live pain-free, suffer-free, and mourn-free lives, but sin has terribly interrupted our destiny.

Read Hebrews 11.

The point of this chapter is not how these great people of faith suffered. The point is that they trusted God through their suffering. It would be grotesque to welcome pain and suffering into our lives, but it is necessary to expect it. Don't call it friend, call it teacher. God doesn't let us suffer out of cruelty. We suffer because we live on a corrupt planet, but it is also in the midst of our poverty and grief that we truly realize our need of a Savior! 2 Corinthians 7:10 says that Godly sorrow brings repentance, which leads to salvation. My pastor relayed the following story of one of his friends:

The Be-Attitudes
How We Can Get Over Ourselves And
Live Lives Approved By God!

On one occasion this friend went to his doctor for a check-up and the doctor asked him, "How are you getting along?"

The man replied, "What do you mean?"

"Your infirmity, your disease, how are you dealing with it?"

The man declared, "I don't see this as an infirmity. I see it as a blessing."

"A blessing? How's that?" the doctor replied.

The man continued, "Are you a Christian?"

"No."

"Well, I am. And I believe that God has allowed me to have this disease for a reason; so I see it as a blessing. In fact, because of this disease I get to speak to people I wouldn't ordinarily have the chance to meet and tell them about Jesus; just like I'm telling you now."

The Be-Attitudes
How We Can Get Over Ourselves And
Live Lives Approved By God!

Wow, that is powerful stuff! This man gets it. He understands that his suffering is a temporary situation, compared to an eternity with God and the glory to be revealed. In the midst of his suffering, he embraces the comfort God brings to him!

Take an honest look at your mourning. What prevents you from trusting God? Pour out your tears and allow Him to fill your void. He doesn't wait in anger, he waits in love.

> *The sacrifices of God are a broken spirit; a broken and contrite heart, O God, you will not despise.* (Psalm 51:17)

Jesus warned us that while we live on this sinful planet we will have trials. God may reveal the purpose for our suffering, or we may never understand why these things happen on this side of heaven. Either ways he promises to be with us and never leave us (1 Peter 1:6, Hebrews 13:5).

The Be-Attitudes
How We Can Get Over Ourselves And
Live Lives Approved By God!

"Therefore also God highly exalted Him, and bestowed on Him the name which is above every name, that at the name of Jesus EVERY KNEE SHOULD BOW, of those who are in heaven, and on earth, and under the earth, and that every tongue should confess that Jesus Christ is Lord, to the glory of God the Father."
(Philippians 2:9-11)

After Jesus suffered, God comforted him and lifted him up. Jesus promises us the same things too, "Blessed are those who mourn, for they will be comforted."

God sent his Son to redeem us from Satan's death-grip. He has a better plan for us than we do. While we live here on earth we can never be totally satisfied. In fact, we shouldn't get too comfortable here; it is temporary. For Jesus' followers our true home is in heaven with him.

Don't allow your trials to make you bitter; they have a purpose. God will use them to make you into the person he

The Be-Attitudes
How We Can Get Over Ourselves And
Live Lives Approved By God!

intended you to be. The comfort which Jesus promises is partially for here and now, but ultimately you will be fully comforted in the arms of The Hearer of Cries.

> *"God will wipe away all our tears and there will be no more death or mourning or crying or pain."* (Revelation 21:4).

"O Love that will not let me go, I rest my weary soul in thee."

The Be-Attitudes
How We Can Get Over Ourselves And
Live Lives Approved By God!

Discussion:

1) Is there something you are mourning about or have mourned over in the past? How has this affected you?

2) Jesus tells his followers to take up their cross and follow him (Matthew 16:24-25). In light of this imperative, how are mourning and suffering to be expected in the lives of believers as they are being conformed into the image of Christ? (See also Isaiah 53:3; Matthew 5:39, 44; Luke 17:25; Luke 24:26 and Hebrews 13:1-3.)

3) Read Romans 5:1-5, 2 Corinthians 1:3-7, and Hebrews 12:2-13. How do these verses give purpose to suffering?

The Be-Attitudes
How We Can Get Over Ourselves And Live Lives Approved By God!

Blessed are the meek, for they will inherit the earth. Matthew 5:5

Meek is not a word we often use to describe a powerful, self-assured person. Someone who is meek might even call up images of being mousy or weak, but that is the complete opposite of what it means to be meek. The Hebrew word for meek means to be humble or lowly, as a servant is in relationship to a king. On the other hand, meek in Greek means powerful strength under control. It is the idea of a wild horse that has been tamed and can now be controlled to serve a useful purpose. Therefore, a meek person is one who serves with controlled strength, a person who doesn't have to be a servant, but one who is willing and able to accept his or her position under someone's authority.

The Be-Attitudes
How We Can Get Over Ourselves And
Live Lives Approved By God!

Jesus was meek. He was the living definition of power under control! Jesus was God in the flesh, yet he emptied himself, he humbled himself and came to earth as a man to save us. He became a servant, even though he had all the authority in the universe to do as he pleased, he subjected his strength and chose to put it aside to rescue us. He obediently accepted God the Father's will for himself and did what was necessary to save us. He was willing to save us, but more importantly he was able to save us.

Because we sin, there is a death penalty judgment against us. Romans 6:23 says, "The wages of sin is death..." The Bible tells us that God requires a perfect, spotless sacrifice, one without defect, to pay for our sins (Leviticus 4:32, 17:11). Therefore, not just anyone could save us, but Jesus was able to save us, because he was perfect and without sin. Had he not been perfect, then his sacrifice would not have been sufficient to pay our death penalty judgment.

Read: John 13:3-12

What an example of meekness Jesus gave to us! He

The Be-Attitudes
How We Can Get Over Ourselves And
Live Lives Approved By God!

also tells us that if we do these things, if we humble ourselves, serving others as he did, then there is a blessing in store for us. God knows how he "wired" us. He knows we are happier people when we help others and are more concerned with other people's needs over our own.

Jesus has all power and authority, yet he uses sinful people to help build his kingdom. Meek people know *they can do all things through Christ who gives them strength (Philippians 4:13)*, yet they are willing to ask others for help. Meek people are not self-absorbed and self-confident; they are Christ-absorbed and Christ-confident.

Those who are meek in spirit are promised a great inheritance: to gain the earth, but what does this mean? To inherit means *to come into possession of or to receive as a right or divine portion*. First and foremost, we don't earn anything from God, because we are entitled or have the right to it. God's grace is a free gift.

The Be-Attitudes
How We Can Get Over Ourselves And
Live Lives Approved By God!

Secondly, *to inherit means to receive from an ancestor as a right or title*. The Bible says, "To all who received him (Jesus), to those who believed in his name, he gave the *right* to become children of God -- children born not of natural descent, nor of human decision or a husband's will, but born of God." (John 1:12)

Therefore, inheriting the earth is given as a divine portion for those who are God's children.

Meek people don't inherit the earth because they've earned it. None of God's gifts are earned or deserved (Ephesians 2:8-9). Meek people inherit the earth because they can be trusted with it, because when we are following Jesus' example of meekness, our own needs are set aside for the good of others and we will have their best interests at heart.

Read: Philippians 2:1-5

There is coming a day when God will establish a new heaven and a new earth; so take note, it will only be inherited and inhabited by God's people!

The Be-Attitudes
How We Can Get Over Ourselves And
Live Lives Approved By God!

Are you willing to accept your position as a servant and serve God and others? Jesus did this for you; how can you not do the same for the King of the Universe? Are you able to serve God and others? No one in his or her own strength is able, but God can *enable* his children to do whatever it is he has called them to do. You must first be willing, and then God's spirit will give you the supernatural power to accomplish the task he has in store for you.

Read: Philippians 4:13

God can make you willing and able, but you must first recognize your spiritual poverty, *Blessed are the poor in Spirit...*, ask Jesus to be your Savior, and then ask him to make you able. This is not a one-time request, it is a lifelong process.

> *Now to him who is able to do immeasurably more than all we ask or imagine, according to his power that is at work within us. Ephesians 3:20*

The Be-Attitudes
How We Can Get Over Ourselves And
Live Lives Approved By God!

Discussion:

1) Read Proverbs 3:5-6, John 1:12 and James 4:7-10. Before you can receive God's blessing, what must you do?

2) Read Matthew 19:14, John 2:13-16, John 10:17-18, 2 Timothy 1:7-9 and 1 Peter 5:1-7. What do these verses teach you about meekness?

3) Read Psalm 37:9, 11, 22, 29, 34; Isaiah 57:13 and James 2:5. What do these verses have to say about a believer's inheritance?

The Be-Attitudes
How We Can Get Over Ourselves And
Live Lives Approved By God!

Blessed are those who hunger and thirst for righteousness, for they will be filled.
Matthew 5:6

Can you imagine never being hungry or thirsty? You'd have to force yourself to eat and drink just to survive. Fortunately, or maybe unfortunately for some of us, this isn't the case. When we hunger and thirst, most of us can readily fill our bodily desire.

This Beatitude speaks to hungering and thirsting for righteousness. Desiring righteous living is not natural. We are born sinful (Psalm 51:5). If you don't believe it, just put two toddlers in a room with one toy and see what happens. Hungering and thirsting for righteousness comes only after

The Be-Attitudes
How We Can Get Over Ourselves And
Live Lives Approved By God!

God makes you aware of your spiritual poverty and he has filled that void, your emptiness, with his Spirit. Only then will your spirit begin to feel the hunger pangs for righteousness.

Read: Genesis 15:6 and Romans 3:22

Apart from Jesus Christ, you will never hunger and thirst for righteousness, because it is Jesus who makes us righteous by his sacrifice on the cross. It's the great exchange! We receive his perfection, he receives our sin. We get the better deal.

Read: Luke 15:11-24

Righteous living is living a life which conforms to God's will; a life which he approves of. The wayward son realized his need only after he was hungry. In fact, it was a direct result of his emptiness and suffering that he was brought to his senses. Only then was he willing to admit his failure, humble himself and then conform to the will of his father.

Picture a potter pressing and shaping a lump of clay to

The Be-Attitudes
How We Can Get Over Ourselves And
Live Lives Approved By God!

conform to his vision of what that clay should become. He presses and pulls the clay, adding and taking away from the lump, until it takes on the form of what he has in mind for it to be. God, our Potter, is also in the process of shaping his people into what he wants us to be. He is about the process of conforming us into the likeness of his Son (Isaiah 64:8; 2 Corinthians 3:16-18).

How do we know what God's will is for our lives? We begin by first knowing and learning what his Word says. It is therein that God reveals himself to us, teaches us truth, and readies us for his service.

> *All Scripture is God-breathed and is useful for teaching, rebuking, correcting and training in righteousness, so that the man of God may be thoroughly equipped for every good work. (2 Timothy 3:16-17)*

Read: Romans 12:1-2

When we hunger and thirst for righteousness, we begin the

The Be-Attitudes
How We Can Get Over Ourselves And Live Lives Approved By God!

process of being restored and perfected into God's image, making us able to serve God and to determine his will for our lives.

God promises to fill us and satisfy us; yet, the desire for righteousness is not quenched. In fact, the more we hunger and thirst for righteous living, the more we find ourselves wanting more and more of it! God satisfies us and fills us with himself, but as we grow closer to Jesus, we'll find ourselves hungering and thirsting for more and more of his righteousness!

Read: John 4:4-15, 7:37-38 and Revelation 7:17.

Jesus wanted the woman to understand there was more to life than earthly needs and concerns, and that he was the answer to all her troubles.

Read: John 6:29-51

The people wanted a sign as great as or greater than Moses and the manna given in the desert, so they could believe in

The Be-Attitudes
How We Can Get Over Ourselves And
Live Lives Approved By God!

him. However, Jesus pointed out that the bread given was from God and not from Moses. Jesus wanted them to understand a deeper truth, that he, Jesus, was the true Bread sent from heaven, and that only in him would they be completely satisfied.

These water and bread verses are the keys to earthly contentment. Only in Jesus, by Jesus and through Jesus do we desire righteousness, and are then satisfied, filled with God! It is wholly the work of the Spirit living within us.

As God controls more of your life, the effects will be seen in the way you think, behave and how you treat others. And not only will you begin to desire righteousness for yourself, you will long to see "right" done in your world.

Only when we let go of trying to control our lives, and allow God to be our God, will we find peace with Him and ourselves. Becoming conformed into the image of Jesus is not an easy process. It can be painful, but it is necessary.

Lord, you are the Potter, I am the clay.

The Be-Attitudes
How We Can Get Over Ourselves And
Live Lives Approved By God!

Discussion:

1) Can you think of a time(s) in your life when your emptiness and suffering made you hunger and thirst for righteousness? Explain.

2) Romans 12:1-2 speaks of presenting yourself as a living sacrifice. What does this mean to you?

3) How does Jesus' sacrifice restore you to your original position of being made in God's image? (See Galatians 4:3-7 and Titus 2:11-14)

4) Read Jeremiah 18:1-6, Romans 8:28-29, Romans 12:2, and 1 Peter 1:14. What do these verses teach you about the purpose of conforming?

5) What does being filled with God look like? (Read Philippians 1:9-11; Ephesians 3:16-19; and Galatians 5:22-25.)

The Be-Attitudes
How We Can Get Over Ourselves And
Live Lives Approved By God!

Blessed are the merciful, for they will be shown mercy. Matthew 5:7

Mercy is almost always linked with grace, but they are different. Grace is God's undeserved favor or kindness to those who don't deserve it. It is a gift given by God and must be received through repentance and faith - turning from sin and trusting in Christ (Ephesians 2:8-9). Mercy, on the other hand, is kind treatment to those who are in trouble or have been rescued from danger, and who may or may not deserve to be shown kindness.

Simply put, grace is *getting* what we *don't deserve*, God's gift of forgiveness; while mercy is *not getting* what we *do deserve*, God's punishment. But his mercy is more than that.

The Be-Attitudes
How We Can Get Over Ourselves And
Live Lives Approved By God!

When we find ourselves in desperate situations outside of our control, it is God, in his mercy, who rescues us.

Being merciful, like being righteous, isn't something that comes naturally. Mercy is something we learn. It is connected to the second Beatitude, *"Blessed are those who mourn..."*, because mourning can be our "Mercy Teacher". As we experience painful times, we learn how important it is to receive kind treatment from others in our time of need. In fact, it is during difficult times that we most often learn more about God's love, faithfulness, forgiveness and mercy.

On one occasion in my adult Sunday school class we divided into small group discussions. One of the questions posed by the teacher was, "How have other people's responses to you during difficult trials helped you or hurt you?" One of the men in my group said that he really hadn't experienced difficult trials in his life, and he felt sort of bad or guilty about that (he is in his late forties). My response was, "Thank God. That is wonderful! Live on." It got me thinking, though, about how important it is during trouble-free times to grow our spiritual roots down deep. Our

The Be-Attitudes
How We Can Get Over Ourselves And Live Lives Approved By God!

tendency is to forget about God when everything is going well, but we must grow our roots deep, by spending time in Bible study and prayer, so when the storms of life come, and for most of us they do come, we will be able to stand firm in our faith.

Read: 1 Corinthians 15:58, 2 Corinthians 1:21-22

I know I have grown more and learned more during difficult and trying times than I ever have when everything was going along just fine. I have also become better equipped to help others in similar situations, which I believe is one of the main reasons God allows hard times in our lives.

Read: 2 Corinthians 1:3-7

This isn't to say that you can't be merciful towards others if you haven't been through similar situations, but those who go through similar painful times can relate to another person's pain in a way that someone who didn't go through the same thing can't understand as deeply.

The Be-Attitudes
How We Can Get Over Ourselves And
Live Lives Approved By God!

Mercy is something we learn, but it is also a vow we must live into. My pastor and friend, Reverend Walter "Lucky" Arnold speaks of growing in our faith by living into our vows. Like the vows people take when they get married, Christ's followers must learn to live into their vows by faithfully serving God and others. Therefore, when we make a confession of faith to God, admitting our emptiness and need of a Savior, and then promising to serve Him the rest of our lives, we must put mercy into action whether we want to or not. We must live into it, because God demands we do (Luke 6:36). We may not know what we're getting ourselves into, but God does, and he promises to sustain us through it (Isaiah 46:4).

Read: Matthew 18:21-35.

Can you imagine behaving like the unmerciful servant in this story? It seems unbelievable, but this is exactly what we do. We have been forgiven of a much greater debt than the servant, yet we are prone to selfishness, envy, anger and an unwillingness to help others. We are quick to be offended when others slight us, yet we expect God's mercy no matter

The Be-Attitudes
How We Can Get Over Ourselves And Live Lives Approved By God!

how we behave. The judgment which Jesus pronounced in this story is frightening:

This is how my heavenly Father will treat you unless you forgive your brother from your heart.

When you truly grasp that it is impossible to repay God for his grace and mercy toward you, it becomes exceedingly easier to forgive those who have hurt and offended you, whether they admit their short-comings or not.

Since we have received God's grace and mercy, we are compelled, no commanded, to do the same for others.

If you want mercy, give mercy.

The Be-Attitudes
How We Can Get Over Ourselves And
Live Lives Approved By God!

Discussion:

1) According to Ephesians 2:1-10 (esp. vs. 7 and 10) what is the purpose in God's extending his grace and mercy toward you?

2) How have you experienced God's mercy?

3) What does being merciful look like in your life? Has your own experience with suffering helped you to be merciful to someone else who is suffering? Explain.

4) According to Hebrews 4:14-16, who is your High Priest? How and when should you come to him?

The Be-Attitudes
How We Can Get Over Ourselves And
Live Lives Approved By God!

Blessed are the pure in heart, for they will see God. Matthew 5:8

When I was a teenager I went to the Bahamas with one of my friends and her family. I'll never forget how crystal clear the water was. It was a blazing, azure blue that could have been two feet deep or two hundred feet deep. The water was so clean and pure you could see right to the bottom of the ocean floor! I couldn't wait for the boat to stop so we could jump in and swim. In contrast, a few years ago my family and I went on vacation in South Carolina and went swimming at a nearby lake. The water was a dark, brownish color. You couldn't see anything beyond an inch deep. Guess which body of water I preferred swimming in? The pure one of course!

The Be-Attitudes
How We Can Get Over Ourselves And
Live Lives Approved By God!

Having pure hearts is closely related to, *"Blessed are the poor in spirit..."*, because we must first recognize our spiritual poverty. Nothing we have to offer God is pure or righteous; none of our thoughts, our intentions or our decisions. God doesn't want us polluted and dirtied by this sinful world. He wants us to live lives that seek out pure living. Trusting in Jesus is the beginning point of having a pure heart, because at the moment we trust in Jesus, God fills us with his pure, Holy Spirit. Only then will we be able to choose pure living!

> *... guard your hearts and minds. Keep your thoughts on things that are good, true and pure. Don't get dirtied by sinful things in this world. Live how God's Word has taught you to live. (Based on Philippians 4:6-9.)*

To guard our hearts and minds is a defensive position of protecting, shielding or defending. To be "on guard" is to watch defensively and to be actively alert to danger. Being "on guard" is to be on the lookout for any threat, like the Secret Service does when they guard the president, watching

The Be-Attitudes
How We Can Get Over Ourselves And Live Lives Approved By God!

for anyone or anything that might harm him. The Bible tells us that we are to be "on guard", against the Evil One, because he is out to destroy us (1 Peter 5:8). We are in a spiritual, unseen battle against evil forces, and we are to protect ourselves like warriors in battle who wear armor to protect themselves against their enemy.

Read: Ephesians 6:10-18

I once took a fencing class with my brother. I had fun until I actually had to fight him. I would begin in the "on guard" position, the stance a fencer takes to get ready to attack and defend, but I would shrink back every time my brother would lunge at me with his sword. Even though I was wearing protective gear, I could never muster enough bravery to face an attack. I knew my brother wouldn't show me any mercy!

This story serves as a reminder to me that Satan shrinks back too, when we face him wearing all of our protective gear, because he knows God will not show him any mercy either – he's doomed already. It's important to note that the armor

The Be-Attitudes
How We Can Get Over Ourselves And Live Lives Approved By God!

pieces from the above passage from Ephesians 6 are all defensive protection, except for one, the Sword of the Spirit, which is the Word of God. It is our "on guard" protection against the Evil One.

The risqué topics on television and in the media that beam down into our homes today are a stark contrast to what was acceptable only ten years ago. Even the subject titles on magazines, now prominently displayed in grocery store check-outs, scream out their vulgarity. God wants his children to be "on guard" for a reason. He knows that when we allow the trash into our lives, little by little, the trash seems more acceptable until we find ourselves like that proverbial toad in the scalding hot water. The water started out cool and gradually grew hotter and hotter until it boiled the toad to death! Don't be like the toad!

Being pure in heart begins the moment you trust Jesus to save you, but it is also a lifelong process of God's conforming his children into the likeness of His Son by obedience to his Word. This battle is not fought alone; Jesus will see you through to the end.

The Be-Attitudes
How We Can Get Over Ourselves And
Live Lives Approved By God!

In the Old Testament the priests would have to purify themselves before entering God's presence. Today, when we clothe ourselves in Christ's purity, by his cleansing blood we can boldly come into his presence and see him.

Read: 1 Thessalonians 5:21-23, Psalm 11:7 and Hebrews 10:19-23.

As you live your life in obedience to God, he gives you the honor and privilege of participating with Him in advancing His kingdom and bringing his salvation and peace to others. The eternal benefit, of course, is seeing God face to face in heaven when you die!

Lord, cleanse my life and make me pure!

The Be-Attitudes
How We Can Get Over Ourselves And
Live Lives Approved By God!

Discussion:

1) Why do you suppose God wants his children to be pure in heart? (See Hebrews 1:9, Hebrews 9:14, Titus 3:1-8 and 1 Corinthians 3:16-17)

2) According to John 16:7-15 and Ephesians 6:10-18, how does God help to equip you in order to stay pure in heart?

3) According to 1 Corinthians 2:16, believers have been given the mind of Christ. This being the case, what responsibility do you think you have?
(See also 1 Corinthians 6:19-20)

The Be-Attitudes
How We Can Get Over Ourselves And Live Lives Approved By God!

Blessed are the peacemakers, for they will be called sons of God.
Matthew 5:9

The Vietnam War raged on during my formative years. It was a tumultuous time with peace rallies, love-ins and anti-war demonstrations held across the country. Thousands of peaceniks were calling for peace, but even the end of the war didn't bring immediate peace to Vietnam. Now the world faces another war, a war against terrorism and an enemy that is not so easily defined and whose borders are not clear.

To our modern ears, *"Blessed are the peacemakers..."* may seem to be the most relevant of all the Beatitudes. In every generation we need peacemakers. I'm quite certain that, for a

The Be-Attitudes
How We Can Get Over Ourselves And Live Lives Approved By God!

Christian, being a peacemaker has to do in part with bringing about peace in the world. After all we are to seek peace and pursue it (Psalm 34:14). But I don't think this is at the heart of what Jesus is talking about here. In fact, he says just the opposite, "...I did not come to bring peace to the earth, but a sword." (Matthew 10:34)

So what kind of peacemakers are we to be?

One of my New Testament professors, a dear man named Dr. Paul Caudill, made it a point to emphasize the connection between grace and peace when studying the Apostle Paul's letters to the church. The Apostle Paul began his letters by writing, "Grace and peace to you..." In response, Dr. Caudill would always declare, "Without God's grace, we cannot have God's peace! God's grace *always* precedes God's peace."

Read: Colossians 1: 21, Romans 5:1, 9-10

Think about this: if you are not "in Christ", then you are an enemy of God. What a terrifying thought! Who can stand if

The Be-Attitudes
How We Can Get Over Ourselves And
Live Lives Approved By God!

God is your enemy? No one, that's for sure!

But, if you are "in Christ", if you've received God's grace and his forgiveness, there is no condemnation, no charge to bring against you (Romans 8:1). You are pronounced, "Not guilty", because through Christ Jesus, the Prince of Peace, the debt for your sin has been canceled (Colossians 2:13-14). You have peace with God; the war against him is over! You have rest for your soul!

Jesus came to bring peace between you and God (1 Timothy 2:5) and peace between you and your fellowman. He is your Mediator. Once you've genuinely become a grace and peace receiver, having become a son or daughter of God, then the natural outcome, or I should say the supernatural outcome, is that you become a grace and *peace* giver, sharing your faith to the faithless and to the faithful.

Read: Philemon 1:6, 1 Thessalonians 5:9-16, and Hebrews 3:13.

The Be-Attitudes
How We Can Get Over Ourselves And Live Lives Approved By God!

When you bring the message of God's grace and peace to your world by leading God's enemies to Jesus and strengthening the bond of peace between fellow believers, you have become a peacemaker.

But what about those troubling statements made by Jesus? *"...I did not come to bring peace to the earth, but a sword."* (Matthew 10:34) Sadly, God's message of peace will not be received by everyone. For some, the very mention of Jesus' name will bring about disdain or outright anger.

There is a conflict raging in our world between good and evil, between Jesus' followers and Satan's followers. This clash between believers and unbelievers extends into our families, our friendships and our acquaintances. Even so, we are instructed to make every effort to live in peace with everyone (Hebrews 12:14).

> *"Peace I leave with you; my peace I give you.*
> *I do not give to you as the world gives. Do not*
> *let your hearts be troubled..."* ~ Jesus ~

The Be-Attitudes
How We Can Get Over Ourselves And
Live Lives Approved By God!

Discussion:

1) According to Jeremiah 6:16, Hebrews 12:14-15, Matthew 7:1-2, 1 Peter 3:8-12 and Proverbs 16:7 how are you to bring about peace in your life?

2) Has being a follower of Jesus resulted in creating conflicts in any of your personal relationships? Explain.

3) What does Colossians 3:12-15 say concerning how you should treat others, regardless of conflict, as a result of your faith?

4) What does it mean to be called sons "children" of God? (See John 1:12-13, Romans 8:13-16, Galatians 3:26-29 and 1 John 5:15.)

The Be-Attitudes
How We Can Get Over Ourselves And
Live Lives Approved By God!

Blessed are those who are persecuted *because of righteousness*, for theirs is the kingdom of heaven. Matthew 5:10

Unlike the previous Beatitudes, this one is conditional. Jesus doesn't pronounce his followers favored for being persecuted for just *any* reason. He says they are favored if they are persecuted specifically *because of righteousness*.

I once had a friend who, after becoming a Christian was wonderfully and obnoxiously zealous about his faith. Don't get me wrong; we should be zealous about our faith. However, his spiritual immaturity caused him to be less than tactful with his co-workers, and he often used his work time

The Be-Attitudes
How We Can Get Over Ourselves And Live Lives Approved By God!

to witness when he should have been working. As a result he was ridiculed for his faith.

"Blessed are those who are persecuted, *because of righteousness...because of me.*" I've often wondered if my friend's co-workers treated him with scorn because of righteousness sake, or was it just his approach and work ethic they found offensive?

This Beatitude is a pivotal point for the rest of Jesus' sermon, because unlike the previous ones, which concern our inner lives and attitudes, this one is a blessing given to those who put those inner attitudes into action. Having become righteous, and being conformed into the image of Jesus, through the power of the Holy Spirit, Christ's followers miraculously become the salt of the earth and lights on a hill (Matthew 5:13-16).

Read: John 15:18-21 and 2 Timothy 3:12-15.

When we live and act like Jesus, it is no surprise that persecution will come from those who are enemies of God.

The Be-Attitudes
How We Can Get Over Ourselves And
Live Lives Approved By God!

(Remember, those who are not "in Christ" are God's enemies.)

When I think of persecution, I think of the martyrs in the early church who refused to denounce their faith and chose to die instead, or I think of Christians in parts of the world today where it is illegal to even own a Bible or gather together with other believers to worship. But Jesus says, "Blessed are you when people *insult you, persecute* you and *falsely say all kinds of evil against you* because of me." (Matthew 5:11-12)

Whatever form of persecution you encounter, if it's because of your faith in Jesus, then you are considered favored and approved by God as a result! He is on your side. You can't lose! Rejoice, because great is your reward in heaven!

Read: Romans 8:35-39

We do not battle alone. Jesus has prayed for us and the Holy Spirit pleads for us. Even when we don't have words for our

The Be-Attitudes
How We Can Get Over Ourselves And
Live Lives Approved By God!

prayers, the Holy Spirit knows how and what to pray for us. Fantastic! (Romans 8:26-39)

Read: John 17:1-24

I love this passage! It is the prayer Jesus prayed right before his arrest and crucifixion. First, he prays for himself, then he prays for his disciples, and then he prays for all those who would eventually believe in him. He prayed for me, and if you are "in Christ", he prayed for you too! Jesus prayed for our protection from the Evil One (vs. 15). He prayed for our sanctification (vs. 17), the process of making us pure and prepared to see him face to face, and he prays that we would be united in our faith (vs.23).

Jesus knowingly faced persecution and death with the knowledge of the glory to come (Hebrews 12:2). He endured the cross for us; in this he found joy, because this gave us our freedom. Jesus was a man of sorrow and acquainted with grief. The way to glory for Jesus was through the cross. There wasn't a shortcut. If we, his followers, are to be

The Be-Attitudes
How We Can Get Over Ourselves And
Live Lives Approved By God!

conformed into his image, we must be ready and willing to do the same.

Read: 1 Peter 2:19-21 and 1 Peter 4:12-19.

Even when we fail at being salty, light-filled Christians, (and we will fail) God will not give up in conforming us into the image and likeness of his Son, because he has promised to never leave us or abandon us. (Hebrews 13:5)

Jesus is coming again. In fact, he is coming in your lifetime! He will either come for you individually in your death, or he'll come for you and his entire church.

Will you be ready?

...Continue in your faith, so that when he appears you may be confident and unashamed before him at his coming.
(1John 2:28 paraphrased)

The Be-Attitudes
How We Can Get Over Ourselves And
Live Lives Approved By God!

Discussion:

1) Jesus encountered persecution before he experienced glory. What ways are you experiencing suffering or persecution before reaching glory as defined by Jesus in Matthew 5:11? Explain.

2) The Psalms hold many promises for God's children in times of trouble. (See a few: Psalm 27:5; 31:14-16; 37:39-40; 46:1; 91:15 and 138:7.)

3) What does it mean to let your light shine before men and why should you? (See Matthew 5:14-16, John 13:34-35 and Ephesians 5:1-20.)

4) What does Isaiah 40:28-31, Galatians 6:9-10 and Hebrews 12:3 have to say about continuing in your service to God?

The Be-Attitudes
How We Can Get Over Ourselves And Live Lives Approved By God!

In closing, I hope this study has helped you to understand the importance of the Beatitudes for your life. I believe they hold the key to emotional and spiritual freedom and the healing that all of us so desperately need. I hope you'll put them into practice so you too will be approved by God!

God's kingdom has begun; the new temple is being built, brick by brick and soul by soul (1 Peter 2:4-10). If you haven't started your Kingdom-journey, you can begin today by following "The Roman Road of Salvation":

Romans 3:10 "There is no one righteous, not even one..."

Romans 3:23 "...for all have sinned and fall short of the glory of God..."

Romans 5:8 "God demonstrates his own love for us in this: While we were still sinners, Christ died for us."

Romans 6:23 "The wages of sin is death, but the gift of God is eternal life in Christ Jesus our Lord."

The Be-Attitudes
How We Can Get Over Ourselves And
Live Lives Approved By God!

Romans 10:9-10 "If you confess with your mouth, Jesus is Lord", and believe in your heart that God raised him from the dead, you will be saved. For it is with your heart that you believe and are justified, and it is with your mouth that you confess and are saved."

Romans 10:13 "Everyone who calls on the name of the Lord will be saved."

Ask Jesus to save you and he will!

K2 -
speed limit the same
hand gun in vehicle
Sexting — underage /
4-R
Gongalez killed w/ fidos
Tyrone White — 17 high school
Rafa George

fire: 20% contain (bike)
on Ft Hood.

→
K2 + other like it
K2 = illegal — marious
speed limits the same day and nite
Handgun — conceal in gun.
Voter — valid ID
2016
Stiffer penalt for human trafficin